# DENTAL

# COLORING BOOK

## BELONGS TO

••••••••••••••••••••••

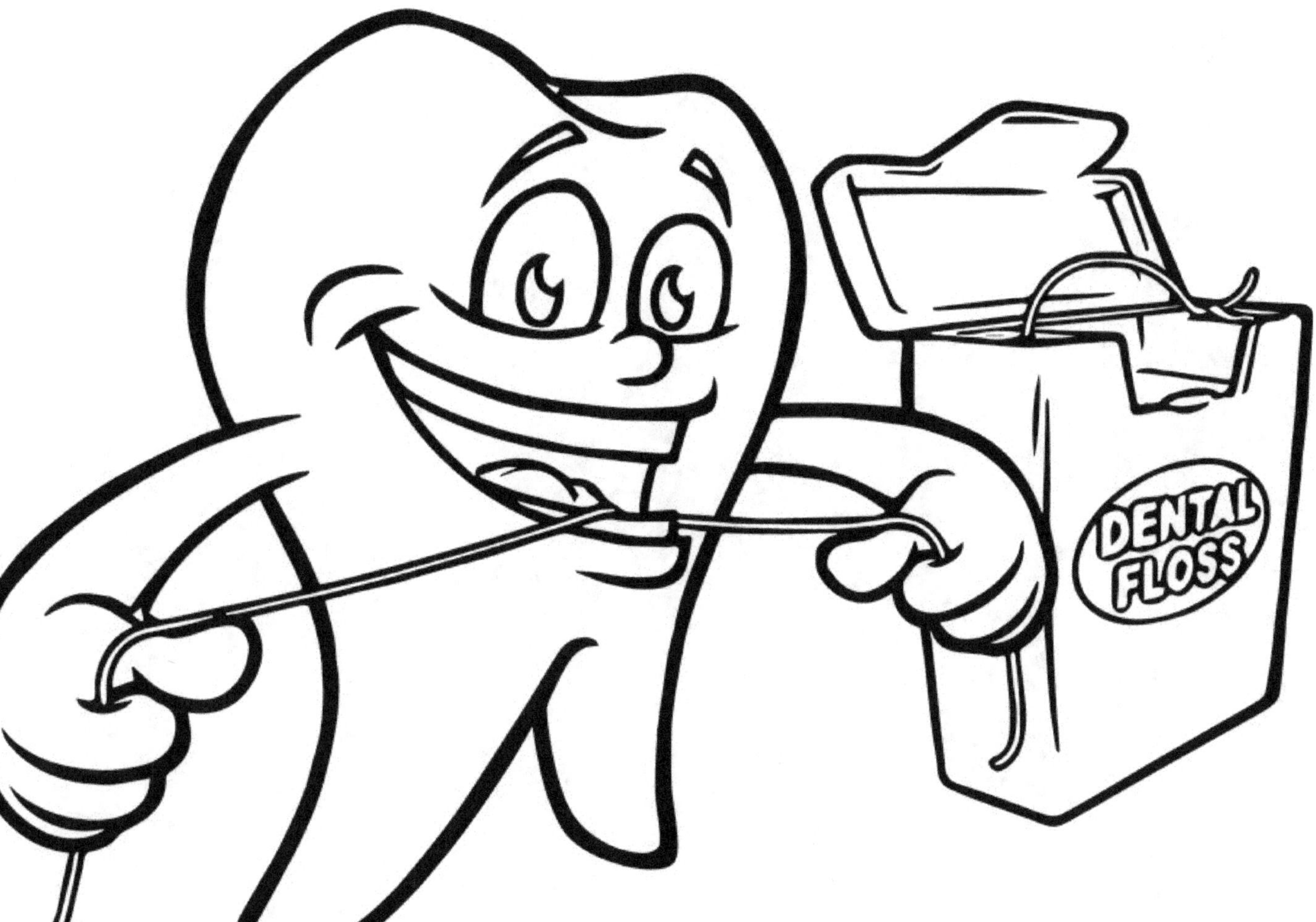
DENTAL
FLOSS

Toot paste
Floss

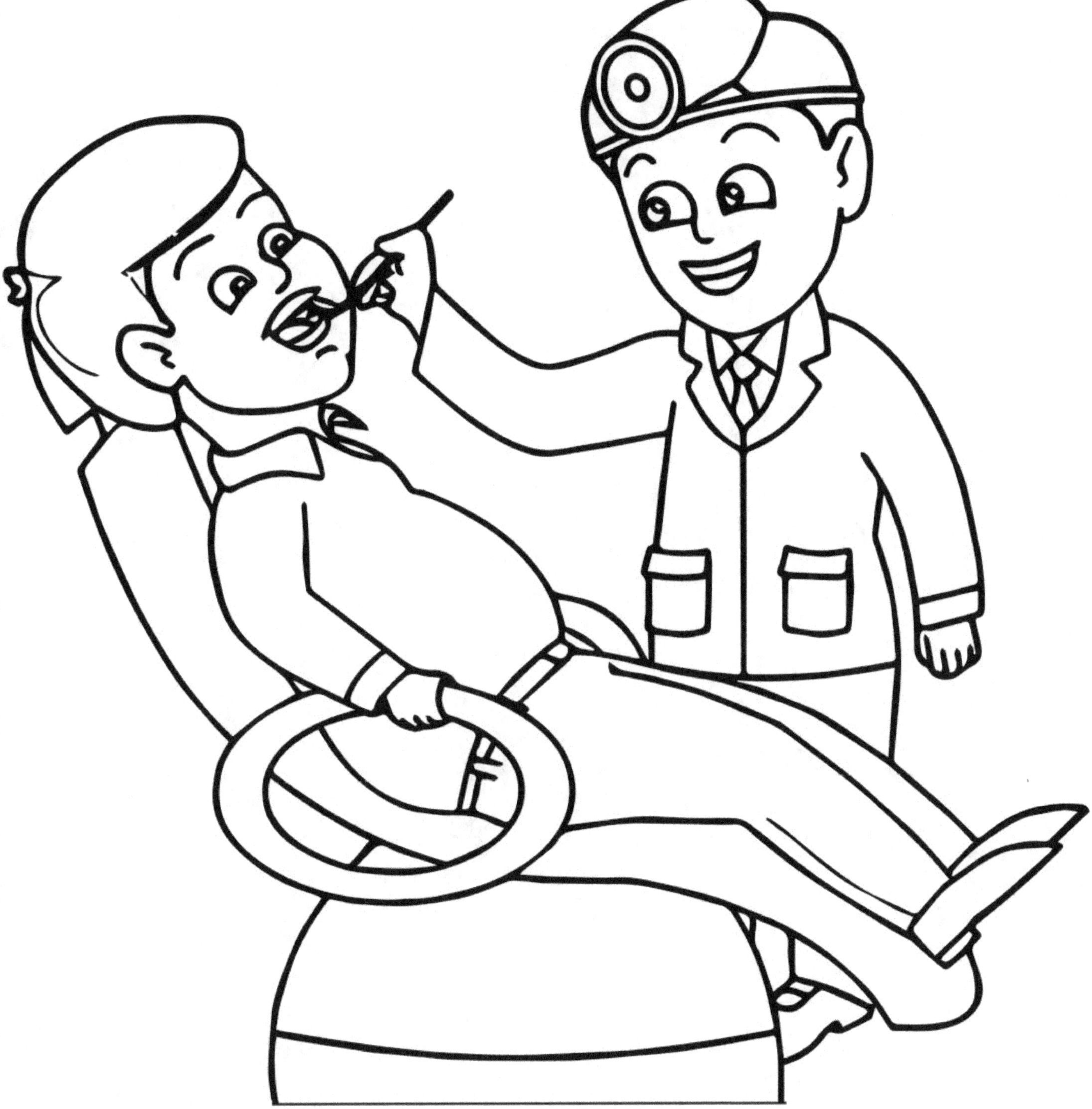

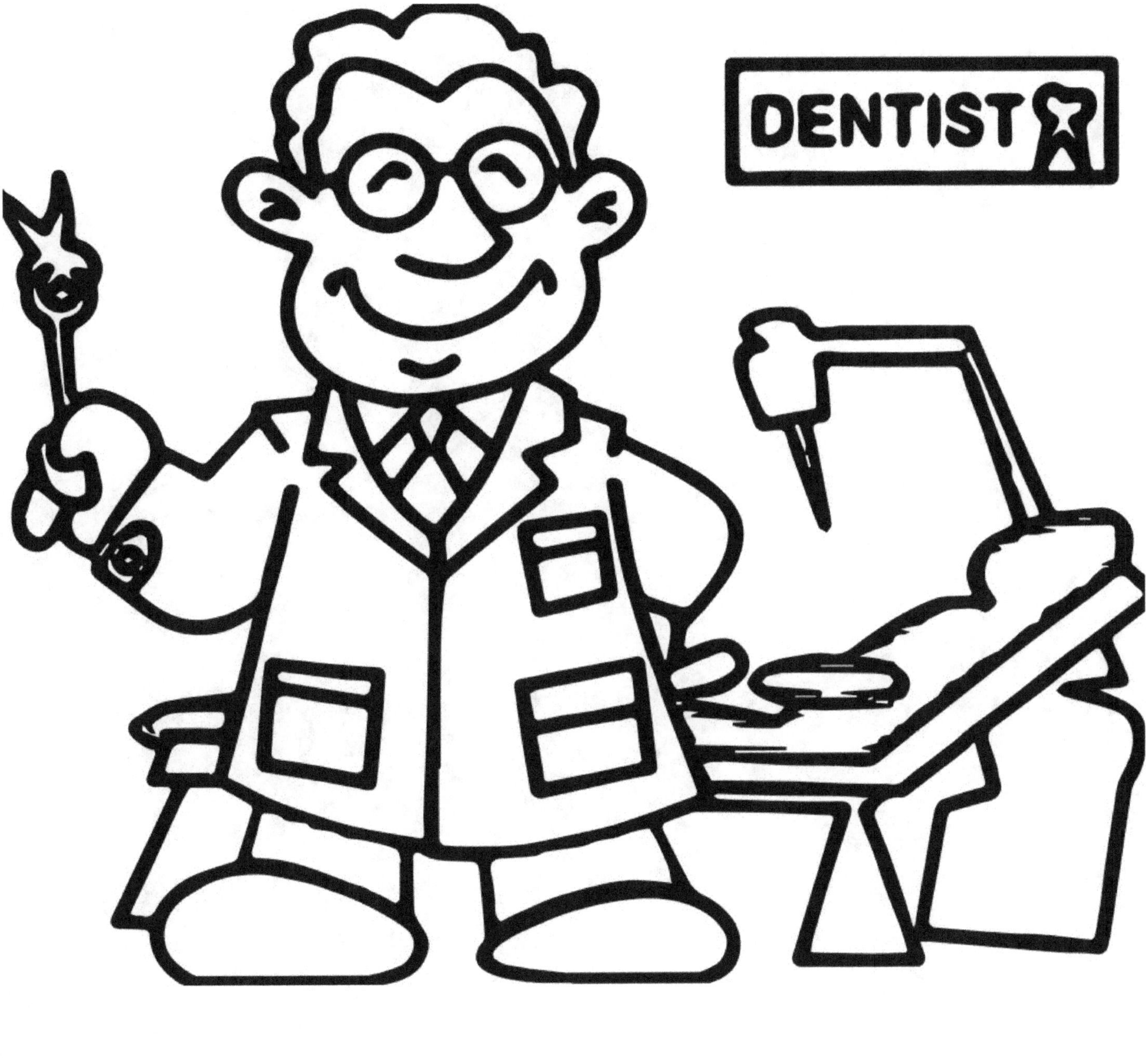
DENTIST

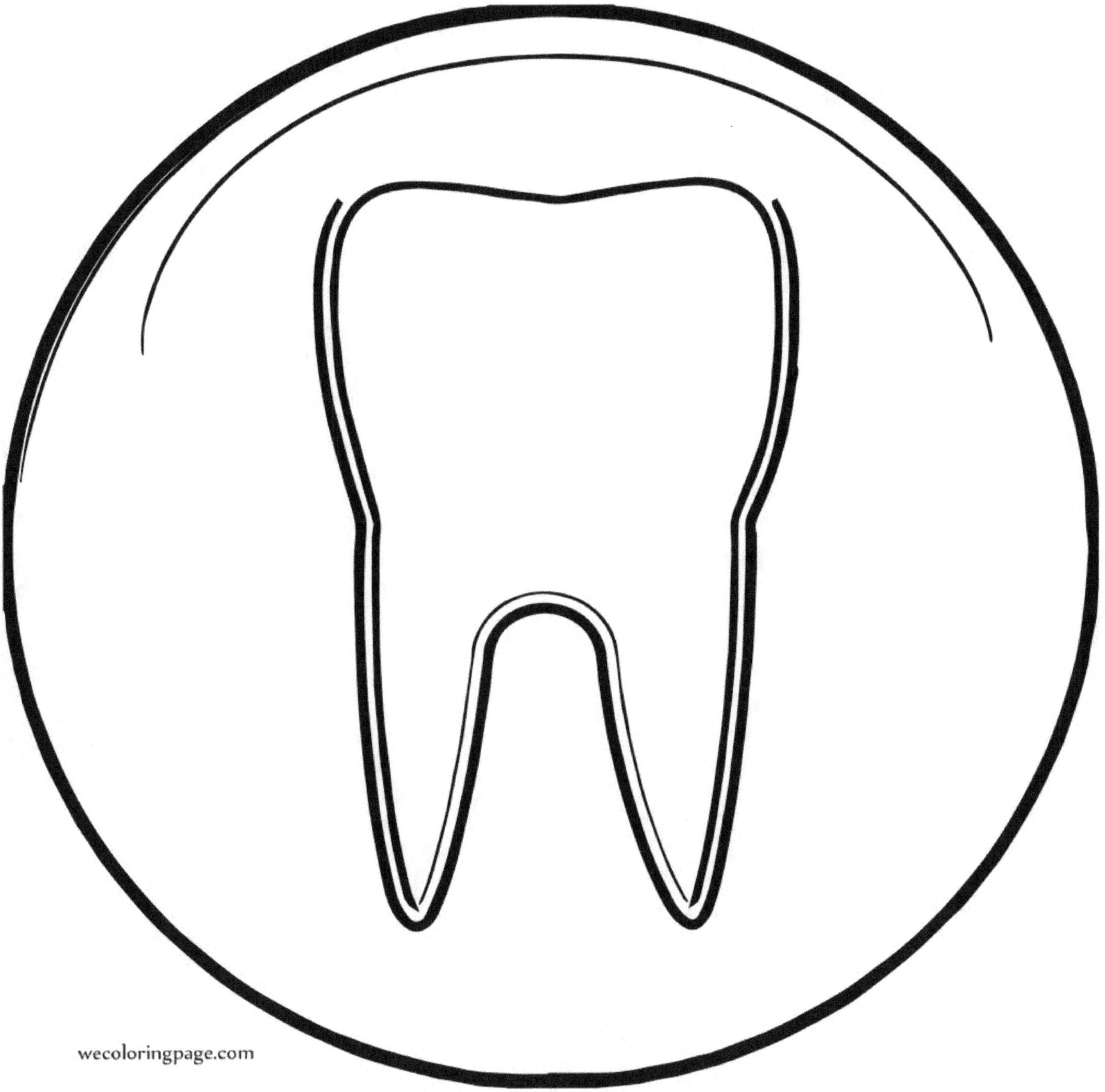

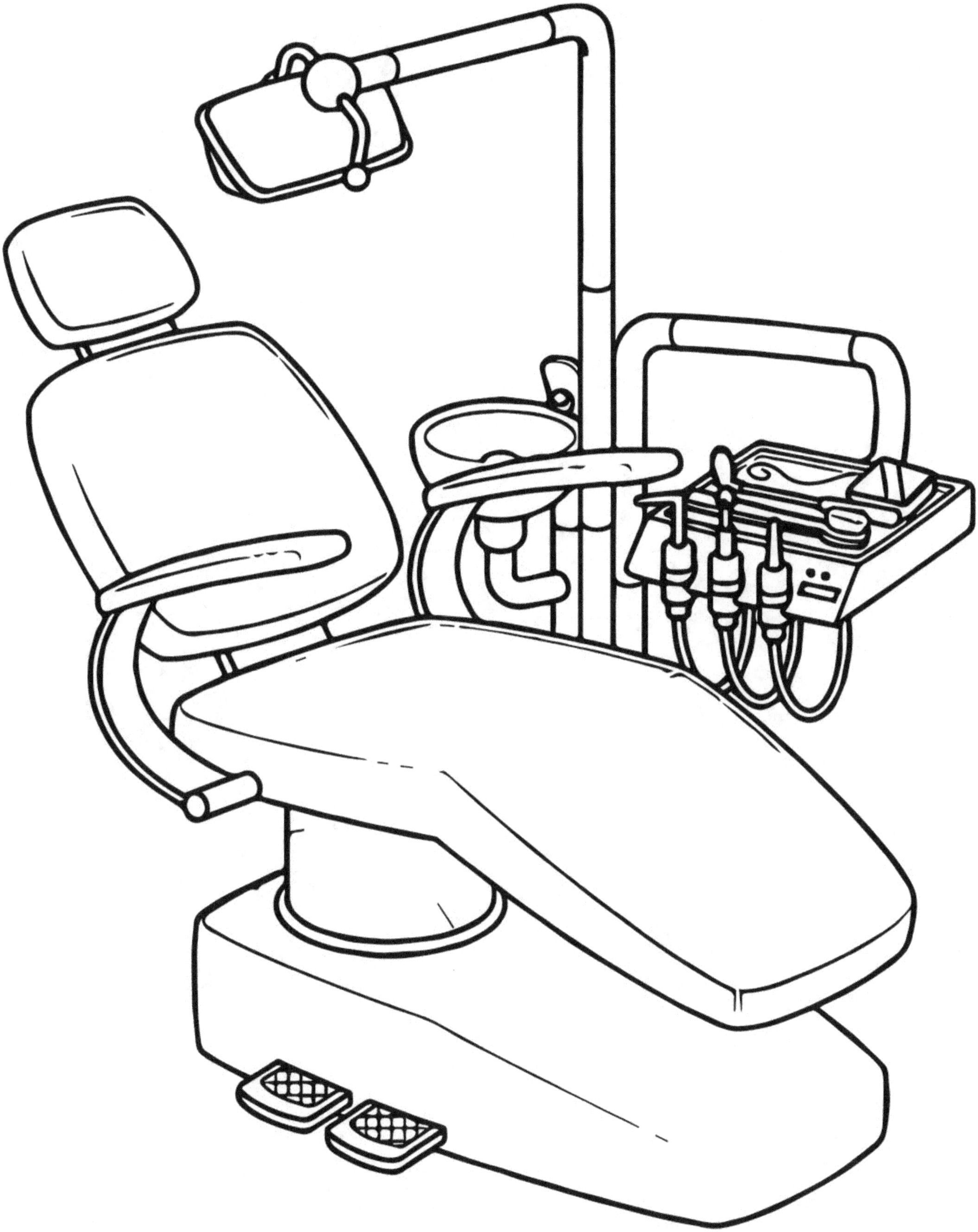

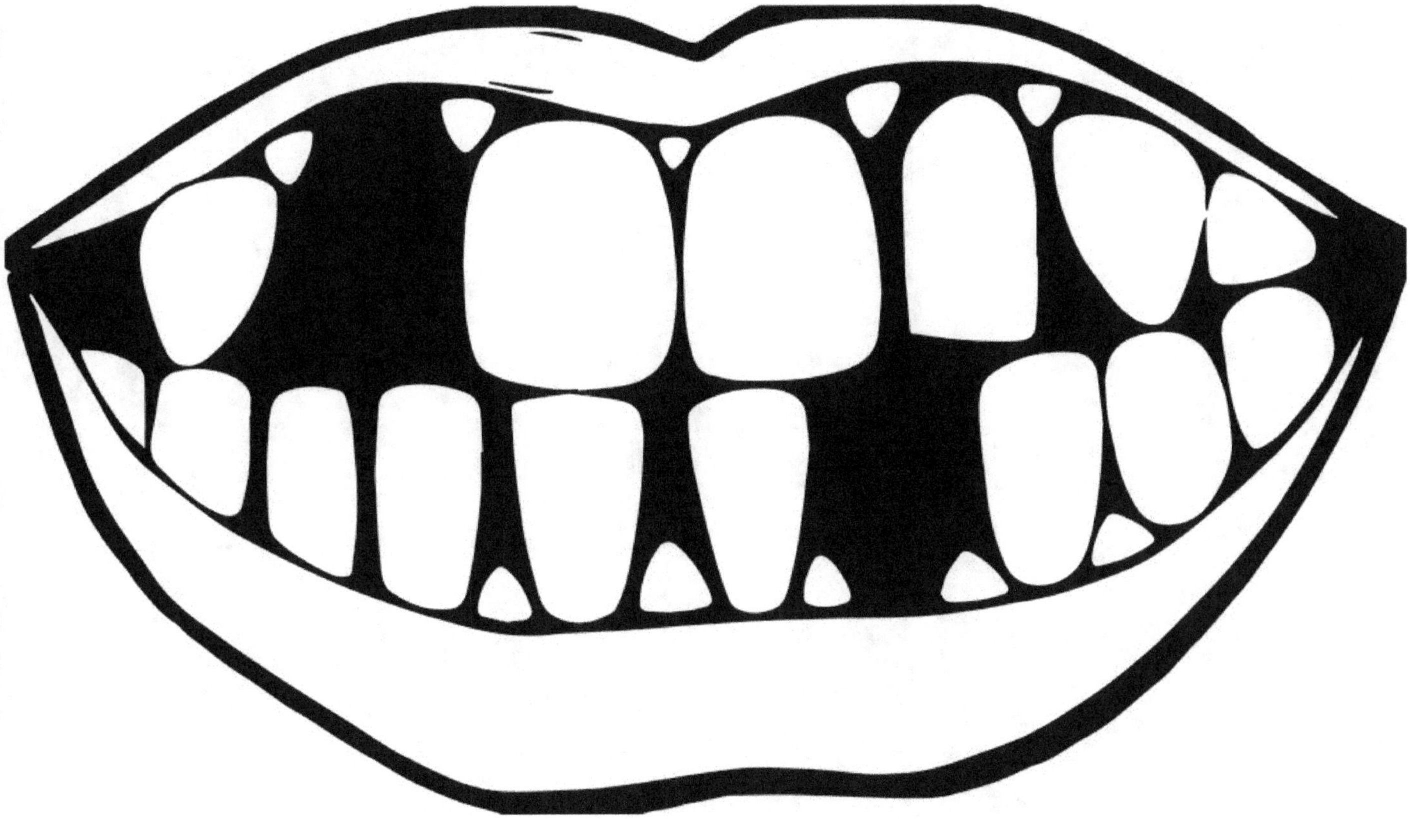

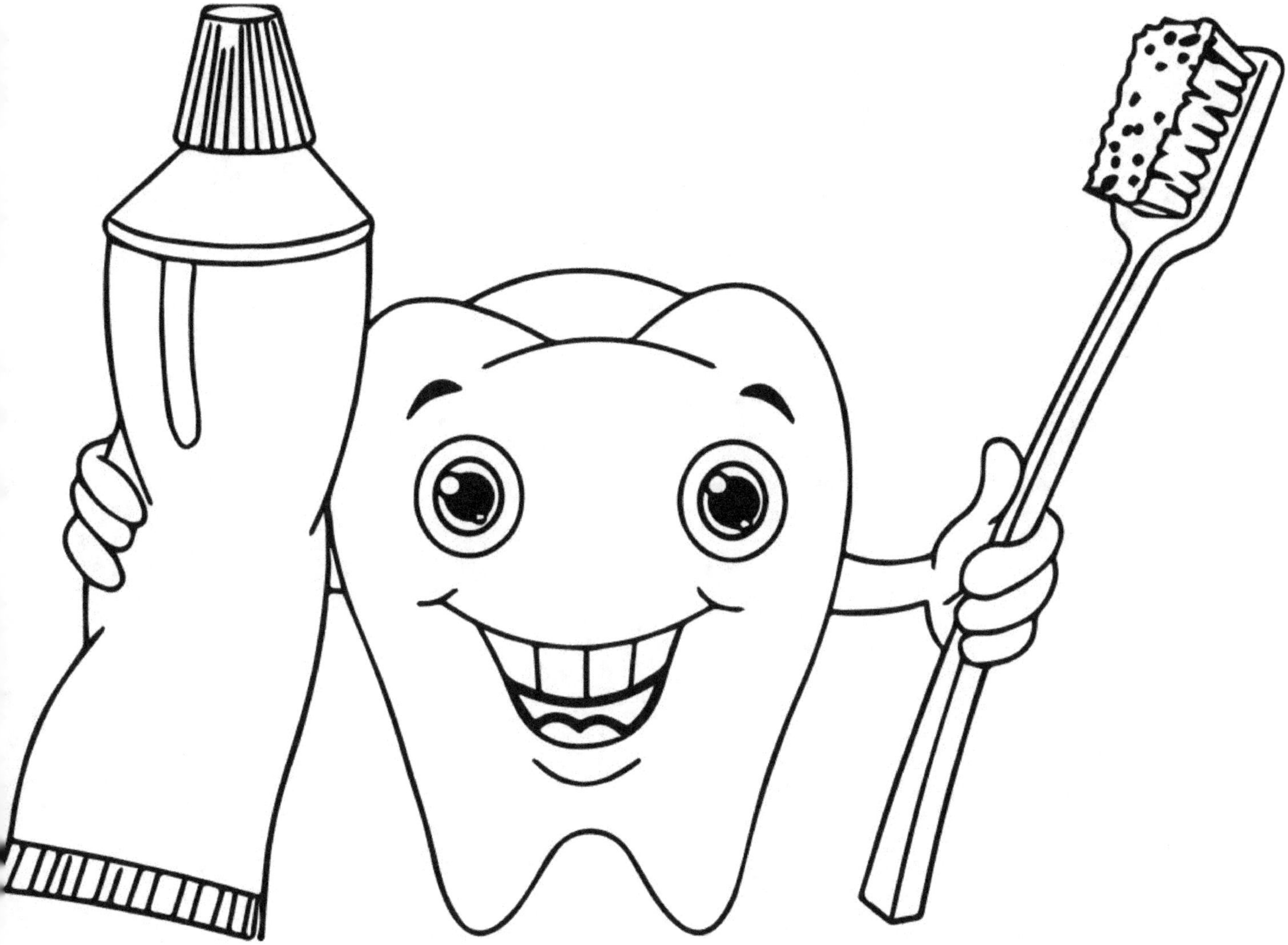

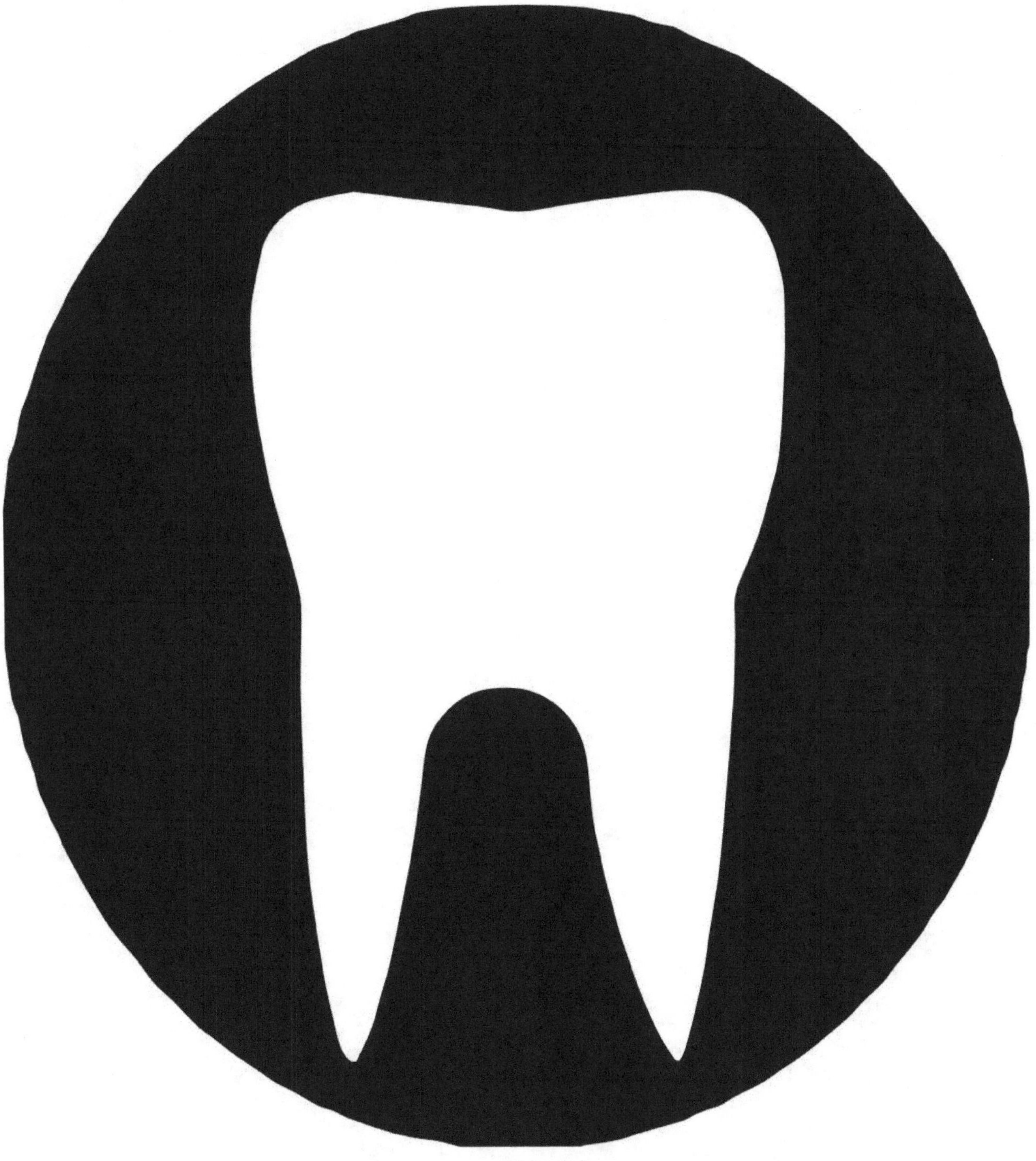

www.ingramcontent.com/pod-product-compliance
Lightning Source LLC
Chambersburg PA
CBHW080815220526
45466CB00011BB/3566
* 9 7 8 1 6 8 7 7 4 2 4 4 5 *